What Makes Me...Me

Written by
**Anne Baldwin
and Levi Baldwin**

Illustrated by
QBN Studios

For all the kids with superpower brains.

Have you ever had a sneeze you just had to sneeze,
or an itch you just had to scratch?

Have your eyes ever blinked or your nose had a sniff,
and it just happened like that?

What about shivers or some scary fears?

For lots of these things, we have no control.

Like when our brains tell our bodies
when to walk or to stroll.

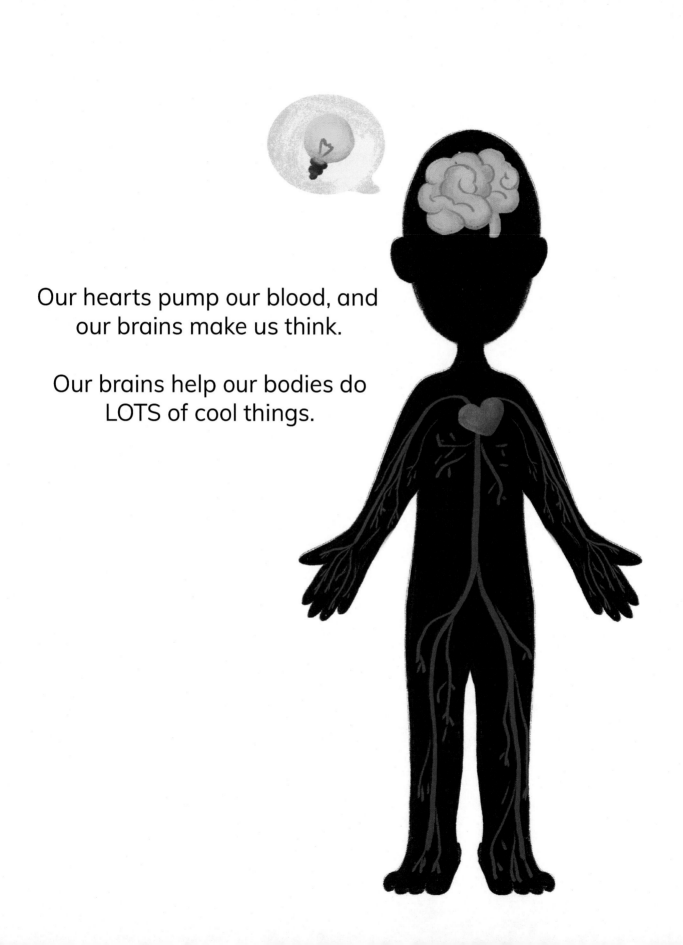

Our hearts pump our blood, and our brains make us think.

Our brains help our bodies do LOTS of cool things.

Our brains help us talk,
to sing,

and to play.

Our brains help us wake up
and feel grateful each day.

Our brains can get angry, get hurt, or get mad.
They can even get worried and then become sad.

Our brains should help us smile and laugh.
But sometimes they don't work quite like that.

My brain is quite silly,
It's wild and free.

Perhaps you were born with
a silly brain just like me.

My brain makes my voice call out strange, funny things.
Sometimes I pretend to fly, imagining wings.

When I play with my friends, we like to climb trees.
I jump from too high and scrape up my knees.

I play with my dog; he's big, brown and white.

When my brain makes me yelp, he gets quite a fright.

My brain tells me to run,
to jump, and to twirl.

I'll wiggle, I'll giggle,
I might even whirl.

I skip and I stomp all
over the place.

I try to walk slowly,
but I like a fast pace!

Then my teachers may scold, they even may yell.

Some people may whisper. Some may stare.

My tics can look funny, but I really don't care.

Sure I may tic and sometimes I twirl.
But despite those things, I'm like any boy or girl.

I'm brave and I'm strong. I'm kind and I'm smart.
I love my family and friends with all of my heart.

The doctor says big words; Tourette, ADHD, and OCD.
No, they don't define me. I won't let that be.

Because what makes me different is special you see.
My brain is my superpower.

It's what makes me.....
ME!

Author Bio

Anne Baldwin lives in Metro-Detroit with her husband Nick and their two boys Levi and Gus. Anne is a fierce advocate for neurodiverse kids and is passionate about stopping the stigma around Tourette Syndrome.

Levi Baldwin lives in Metro-Detroit with his parents, brother, 3 cats, and his leopard gecko named Cool Colors. Levi was diagnosed with Tourette Syndrome at 5 years old and wants people to know that every kid is special and unique even if they may look or act differently.

Illustration Company

QBN Studios is a small Illustration Studio located in Vernon Connecticut. Owners Quynh Nguyen and Christopher MacCoy are passionate about helping authors fulfill their dreams and bring their words to life. QBN Studio's goal is to create an immersive experience for their audiences to tumble headfirst into imaginary worlds. Follow us on Instagram @qbnstudios for the latest updates on illustrations, books, and other projects.

Made in the USA
Monee, IL
07 March 2022